ASTROLOGY

CANCER

BY ABBY DOTY

Apex is distributed by North Star Editions:
sales@northstareditions.com | 888-417-0195

Produced for Apex by Red Line Editorial.

Photographs ©: Shutterstock Images, cover (illustration, constellation), cover (background), 1, 6, 7, 9, 12–13, 14–15, 16–17, 18, 20–21, 22–23, 25, 26, 27, 29; iStockphoto, 4–5, 10–11

Library of Congress Control Number: 2025939149

ISBN
979-8-89250-782-0 (hardcover)
979-8-89250-811-7 (paperback)
979-8-89250-868-1 (ebook pdf)
979-8-89250-840-7 (hosted ebook)

Printed in the United States of America
Mankato, MN
012026

NOTE TO PARENTS AND EDUCATORS

Apex books are designed to build literacy skills in striving readers. Exciting, high-interest content attracts and holds readers' attention. The text is carefully leveled to allow students to achieve success quickly. Additional features, such as bolded glossary words for difficult terms, help build comprehension.

TABLE OF CONTENTS

CHAPTER 1
THE CRAB 4

CHAPTER 2
SUMMERTIME SIGN 10

CHAPTER 3
ABOUT CANCER 16

CHAPTER 4
STRONG BONDS 22

COMPREHENSION QUESTIONS • 28
GLOSSARY • 30
TO LEARN MORE • 31
ABOUT THE AUTHOR • 31
INDEX • 32

CHAPTER 1

THE CRAB

Cancer is a **constellation**. It has five main stars. They form a Y shape. Some people say they look like a crab.

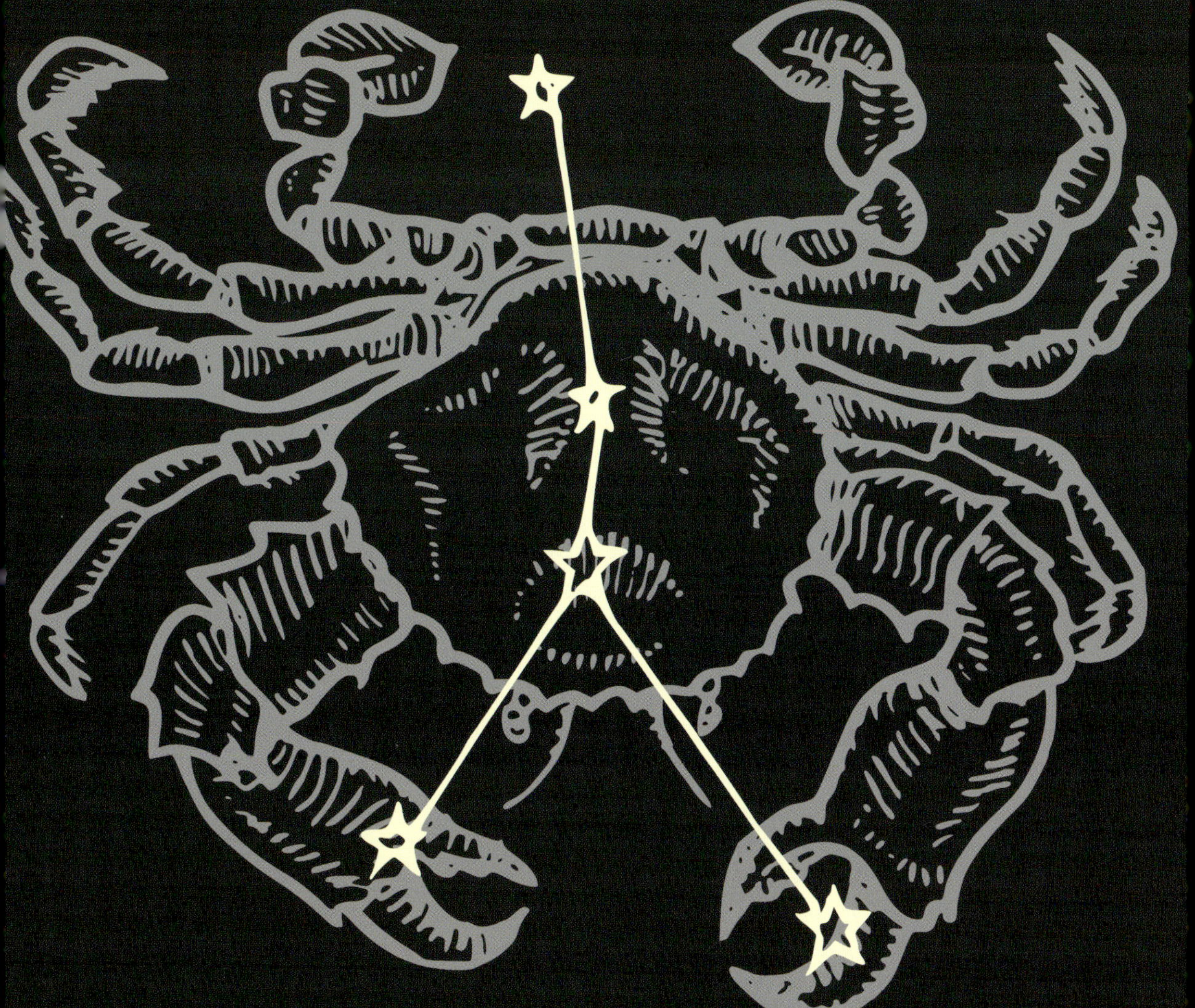

The ends of Cancer's Y shape are said to be the crab's claws.

Ptolemy made a list of constellations. Maps or charts show where they appear in the sky.

Ptolemy wrote about this constellation. He was a Greek thinker from the 100s CE. Other people also studied it. Some gave it different names.

MANY NAMES

The name *Cancer* comes from the Latin word for "crab." In ancient Egypt, people said the stars were a scarab beetle. In Mesopotamia, people said they looked like a tortoise.

The scarab beetle was an important part of religion in ancient Egypt.

The Greeks told a **myth** about Cancer. The goddess Hera sent a crab after the hero Heracles. He killed it. So, Hera placed the crab in the night sky.

FAST FACT

Hera sent the crab while Heracles was fighting a monster. The hero still won the fight.

Heracles was a tough hero who fought many monsters. ▶

CHAPTER 2

SUMMERTIME SIGN

Cancer is one of the 12 **zodiac** signs. Each sign is based on a constellation. It's also paired with a part of the year. This part lasts about one month.

The zodiac signs go in a set order. Cancer comes fourth.

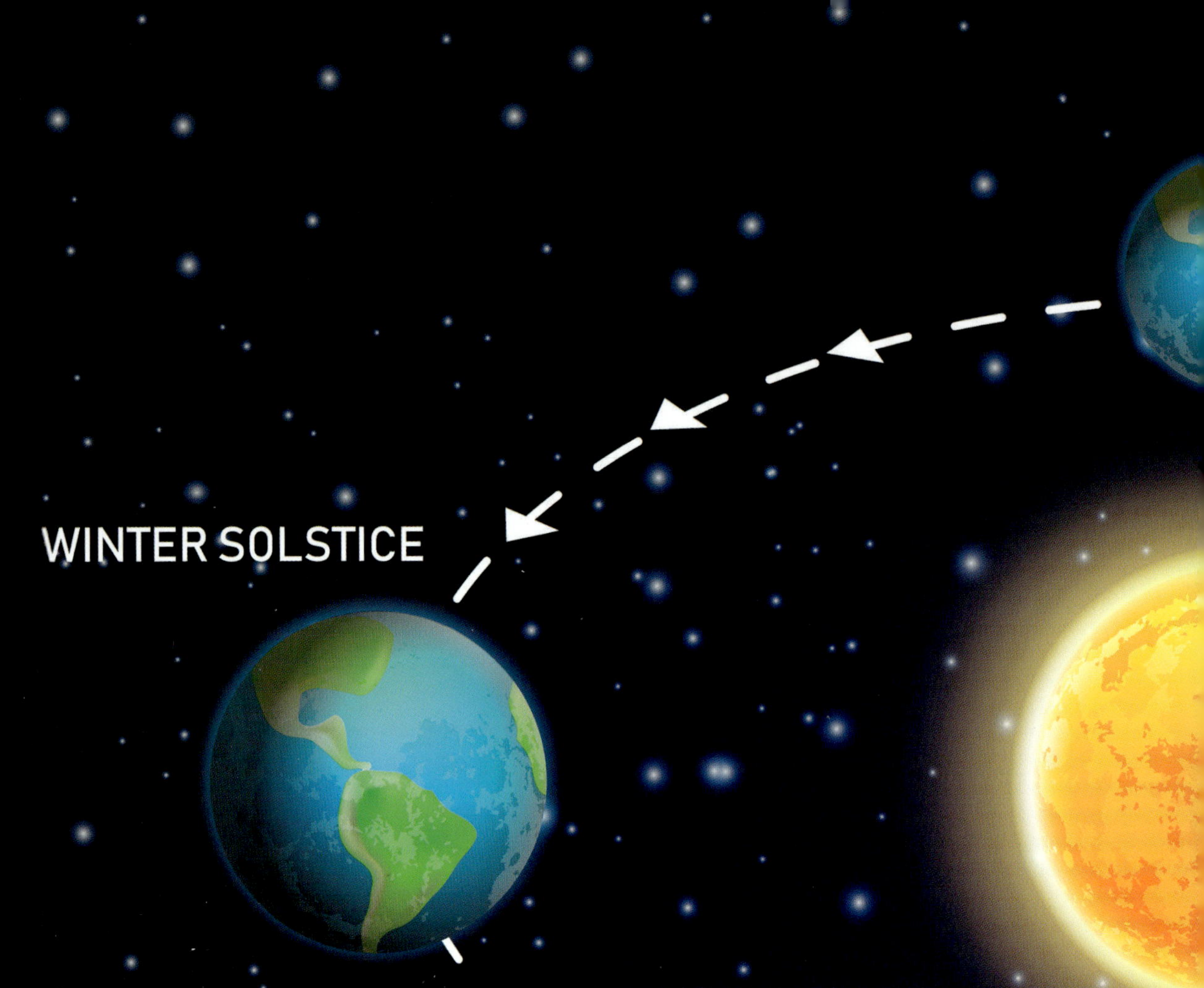

Cancer's time starts around June 22. It begins on the **summer solstice** for the northern **hemisphere**. And it ends around July 22.

Solstices happen because Earth is tilted as it moves around the sun.

FAST FACT

In the southern hemisphere, the summer solstice is in December.

People born during this time are called Cancerians. In astrology, people's signs are said to shape how they think and act. For example, Cancer is linked with being **sensitive**.

WARM AND SUNNY

Cancer is one of three signs matched with summer. Leo and Virgo are the others. All three signs are linked to being friendly and caring. These traits match the sunny season.

People born during Cancer's time have Cancer as their sun sign. Astrology says that sun signs shape the core of who people are.

CHAPTER 3

ABOUT CANCER

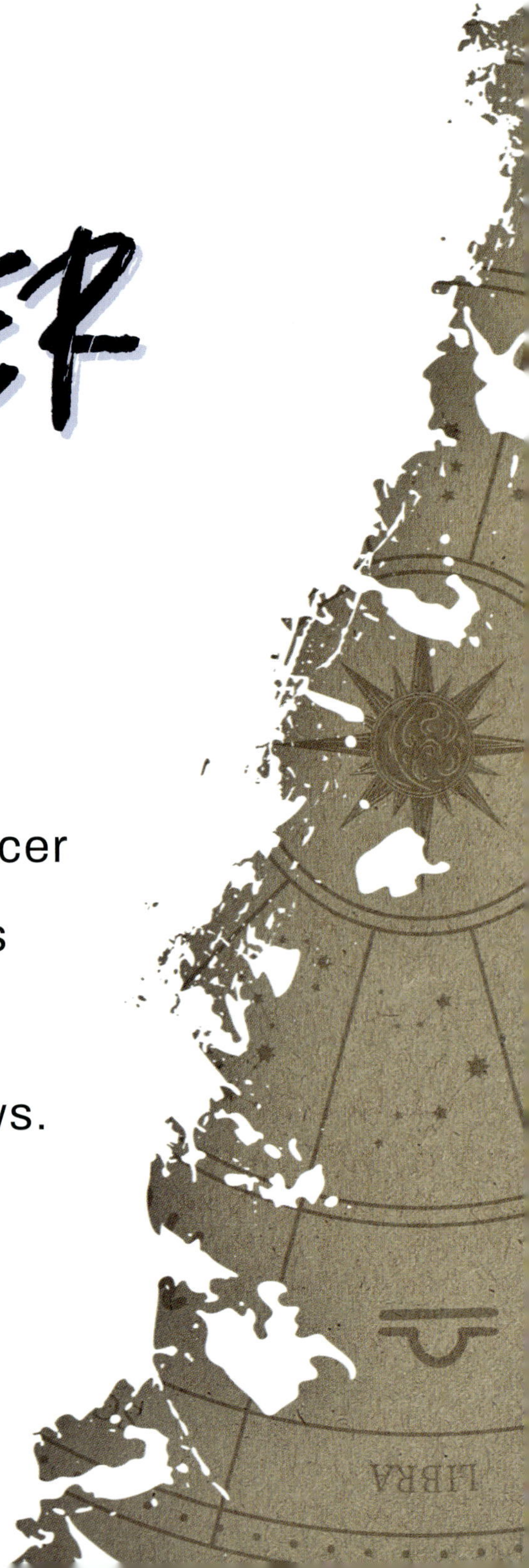

The **symbol** for Cancer looks like two sixes turned sideways. They represent the crab's claws.

Each zodiac sign has a written symbol that represents it. These symbols are sometimes called glyphs.

Cancer's **element** is water. Water is often a symbol of emotion. So, Cancerians are said to feel things deeply. They also pick up on the feelings of others.

FAST FACT

The other two water signs are Scorpio and Pisces.

Like waves, emotions come and go. They can also be very powerful.

Most zodiac signs have a ruling planet. Astrology says this planet shapes how people act. But Cancer is ruled by the moon. The moon often represents change.

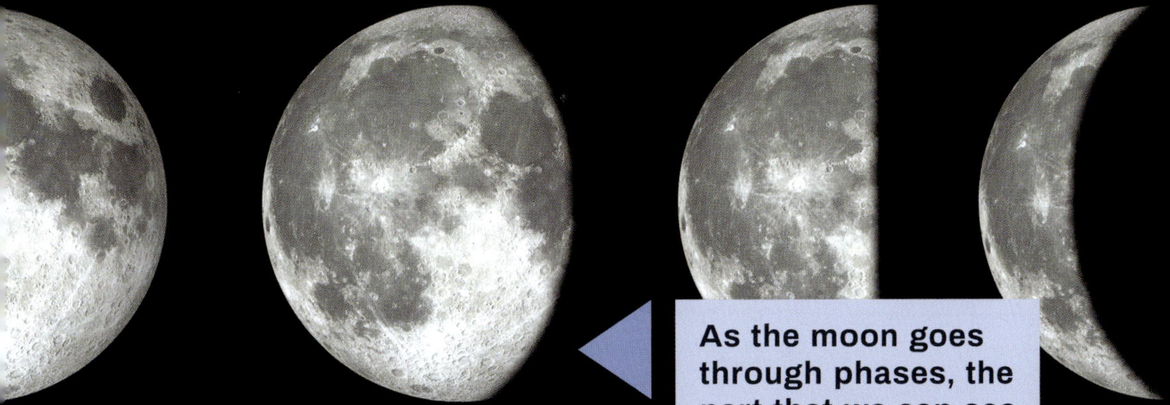

As the moon goes through phases, the part that we can see from Earth grows and shrinks.

THE MOON

The moon goes through phases each month. Its shape in the sky changes. Many myths link the moon to mothers or goddesses. As a result, it also has ties to comfort and caring.

CHAPTER 4

STRONG BONDS

Cancerians are said to be good at understanding other people. They may form deep friendships.

In astrology, the sign Cancer is linked with being a good listener.

At the same time, Cancerians can be introverts. They may have small groups of close friends. And they may often want to spend time by themselves.

FAST FACT

Famous Cancerians include Selena Gomez, Post Malone, and Ariana Grande.

Ariana Grande (right) became close friends with co-star Cynthia Erivo while filming *Wicked*. ▶

Cancerians may be very close to their families.

Cancerians may take time to get close to people. But once they do, they are loyal. They will work hard to protect their friends and families.

Like some crabs, Cancerians may be shy at first. They may use tough "shells" to hide their feelings.

KEEPING IT IN

Some Cancerians have a hard time talking about their feelings. They may want to avoid fights. However, keeping their feelings in can make people more upset.

COMPREHENSION QUESTIONS

Write your answers on a separate piece of paper.

1. Write a few sentences explaining the main ideas of Chapter 2.

2. Do you find it easy to notice what other people are feeling? Why or why not?

3. What season is Cancer linked with?

- **A.** spring
- **B.** summer
- **C.** fall

4. Why could keeping their feelings in make people more upset?

- **A.** The feelings could just grow bigger.
- **B.** The feelings could fade very quickly.
- **C.** People can't control their feelings.

5. What does **introverts** mean in this book?

*At the same time, Cancerians can be **introverts**. They may have small groups of close friends.*

- **A.** people who always love being in big groups
- **B.** people who prefer small, quiet groups
- **C.** people who never have any friends

6. What does **protect** mean in this book?

*But once they do, they are loyal. They will work hard to **protect** their friends and families.*

- **A.** keep people safe
- **B.** push people away
- **C.** hurt people badly

Answer key on page 32.

GLOSSARY

constellation
A group of stars that form a shape.

element
One of four forces (air, earth, fire, or water) that each zodiac sign is matched with and said to be shaped by.

hemisphere
One half of planet Earth.

myth
A well-known story from the past that often includes magic.

sensitive
Likely to have many feelings and share the feelings of others.

summer solstice
The day each year when one of Earth's poles is tilted closest to the sun.

symbol
A thing that stands for and reminds people of something else.

zodiac
The set of 12 signs used in astrology, based on a part of the sky that the sun appears to move through each year.

TO LEARN MORE

BOOKS

Goldstein, Margaret J. *Mysteries of Stars*. Lerner Publications, 2021.

Lee, Jean Kuo. *Chang'e: Goddess of the Moon*. Abdo Publishing, 2023.

Loh-Hagan, Virginia. *Star Signs*. Cherry Lake Publishing, 2021.

ONLINE RESOURCES

Visit **www.apexeditions.com** to find links and resources related to this title.

ABOUT THE AUTHOR

Abby Doty is a writer, editor, and booklover from Minnesota. Her sun sign is Aquarius.

INDEX

C

constellation, 4, 6, 10
crab, 4, 7–8, 16

E

Egypt, 7
element, 19

F

famous Cancerians, 24
feelings, 19, 27
friends, 22, 24, 26

H

Heracles, 8

M

Mesopotamia, 7
moon, 20–21
myths, 8, 21

P

Ptolemy, 6

R

ruling planet, 20

S

sensitive, 14
summer solstice, 12–13
symbols, 16, 19

W

water, 19

Z

zodiac, 10, 20

ANSWER KEY:
1. Answers will vary; 2. Answers will vary; 3. B; 4. A; 5. B; 6. A